ONE-DOLLAR BILLS

BY MADDIE SPALDING

The Child's World®
childsworld.com

Published by The Child's World®
1980 Lookout Drive • Mankato, MN 56003-1705
800-599-READ • www.childsworld.com

Photographs ©: Brian McEntire/Shutterstock Images, cover
(foreground), cover (background), 1 (foreground), 1 (background);
Shutterstock Images, 5 (top), 10, 13; iStockphoto, 5 (bottom), 6, 7,
9, 20 (middle), 20 (bottom); Everett Historical/Shutterstock Images,
15; Old Paper Studios/Alamy, 17, 20 (top); Joe Cicak/iStockphoto,
19

Design Elements: Brian McEntire/Shutterstock Images; Ben Hodosi/
Shutterstock Images

ISBN 9781503820074
LCCN 2016960499

Printed in the United States of America
PA02336

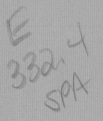

E
332.4
SPA

ABOUT THE AUTHOR

Maddie Spalding writes and
edits children's books. She lives in
Minnesota.

TABLE OF CONTENTS

CHAPTER ONE

WHAT IS A ONE-DOLLAR BILL?

One-dollar bills are a type of money. Four quarters make one dollar. The Bureau of Engraving and Printing makes dollar bills. Bills are made from cotton and **linen**.

Why do you think bills are made from cotton and linen, and not from paper?

Four quarters make one dollar.

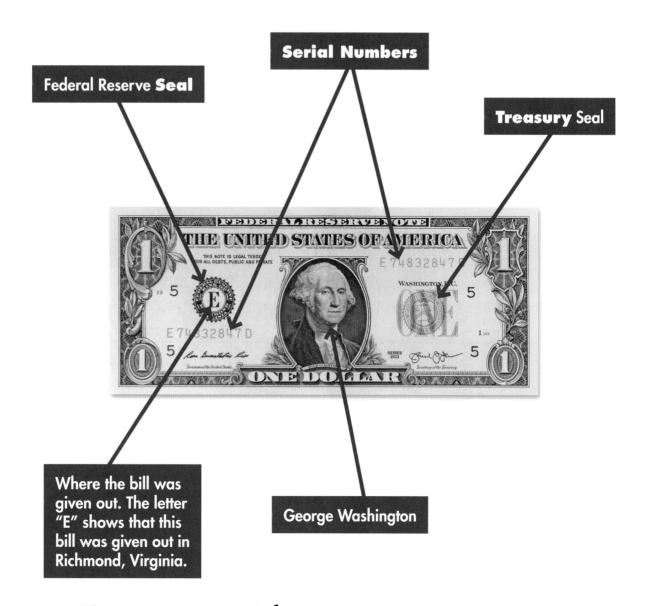

Serial Numbers

Federal Reserve Seal

Treasury Seal

Where the bill was given out. The letter "E" shows that this bill was given out in Richmond, Virginia.

George Washington

Former president George Washington is on the front of the one-dollar bill.

The Great Seal

A pyramid and an eagle are
on the back. They make up the
Great Seal of the United States.

CHAPTER TWO

SECURITY FEATURES

One-dollar bills have serial numbers. Each bill has a different serial number.

Why do you think each one-dollar bill has a different serial number?

There are green numbers on a one-dollar bill.
These are called serial numbers.

The main U.S. Department of the Treasury
building is located in Washington DC.

There are two seals on the front of the one-dollar bill. One is the U.S. Department of the Treasury seal.

Another seal shows the bank that gave out the bill. These details make it more difficult for people to make fake bills.

One bank that gives out bills is in New York City, New York.

13

CHAPTER THREE

THE HISTORY OF THE ONE-DOLLAR BILL

The first U.S. one-dollar bills were made in 1862. Salmon P. Chase was on the front. He was the Secretary of the Treasury. He helped the government handle money.

Salmon P. Chase was the U.S. Secretary of the Treasury during the U.S. Civil War (1861–1865).

George Washington was put on the one-dollar bill in 1869. His wife, Martha, replaced him in 1886.

Martha Washington was the first woman to appear on the one-dollar bill.

George Washington was again put on the one-dollar bill in 1923. The Great Seal was put on the back in 1963. It has two sides. One side has an image of an eagle. The other side has a pyramid. The Great Seal represents the United States's independence.

GEORGE WASHINGTON

was the first president of the United States (1789–1797). He was one of the Founding Fathers of the United States.

1886 U.S. one-dollar bill

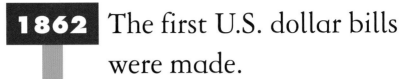 The first U.S. dollar bills were made.

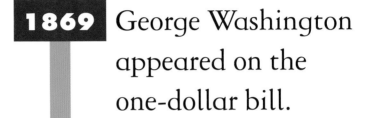 George Washington appeared on the one-dollar bill.

1886 Martha Washington replaced George Washington.

1923 U.S. one-dollar bill

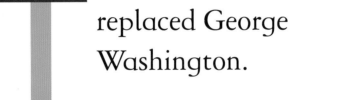 George Washington was again put on the one-dollar bill.

Back of the 1963 U.S. one-dollar bill

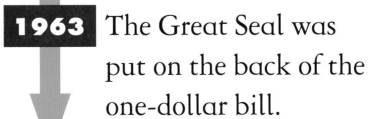 The Great Seal was put on the back of the one-dollar bill.

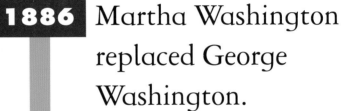

FAST FACTS

★ The one-dollar bill is the cheapest note to make. It costs the U.S. Treasury 4.9 cents to make each one-dollar bill.

★ The average one-dollar bill lasts 5.8 years.

★ More than 10 billion one-dollar bills are made in the United States each year.

★ Two other U.S. presidents have appeared on the one-dollar bill. Abraham Lincoln and Ulysses S. Grant were both on the one-dollar bill from 1899 to 1923.

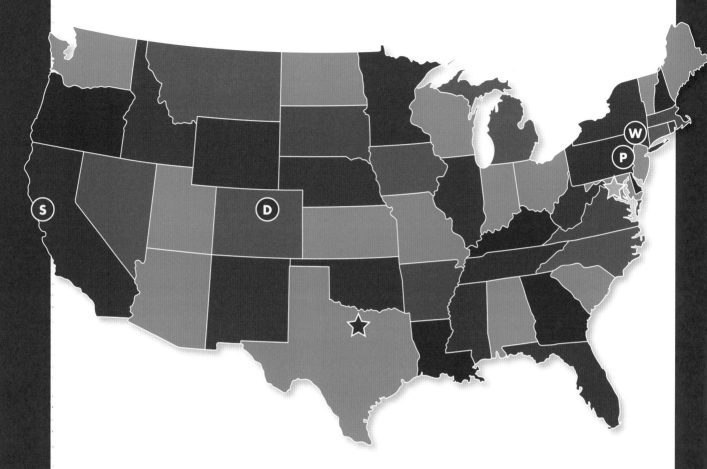

BUREAU OF ENGRAVING AND PRINTING OFFICES

★ Fort Worth, Texas

★ Washington, DC

COIN-PRODUCING MINTS

D Denver, Colorado—Produces coins marked with a D.

P Philadelphia, Pennsylvania—Produces coins marked with a P.

S San Francisco, California—Produces coins marked with an S.

W West Point, New York—Produces coins marked with a W.

linen (LIN-uhn) Linen is a strong type of cloth. One-dollar bills are made from cotton and linen.

seal (SEEL) A seal is an image that is used on official government documents. The Great Seal of the United States is on the back of the one-dollar bill.

serial numbers (SEER-ee-ull NUM-burz) Serial numbers are numbers that identify something. One-dollar bills have serial numbers.

Treasury (TREZH-ur-ee) A treasury is a part of a government that is in charge of a country's money. The U.S. Department of the Treasury is in charge of money in the United States.

IN THE LIBRARY

Dowdy, Penny. *Money*. New York, NY: Crabtree, 2009.

Hamilton, Robert M. *Dollar Bills!* New York, NY: PowerKids, 2016.

Schuh, Mari C. *Counting Money*. Minneapolis, MN: Bellwether, 2016.

Wingard-Nelson, Rebecca. *How Many Pennies Make a Dollar?* Berkeley Heights, NJ: Enslow Elementary, 2010.

ON THE WEB

Visit our Web site for links about
one-dollar bills: **childsworld.com/links**

Note to Parents, Teachers, and Librarians: We routinely verify our Web Links to make sure they are safe and active sites. So encourage your readers to check them out!

INDEX